TERRACES OF RAIN

An Italian Sketchbook

Poems by David St. John

Drawings by Antoine Predock

A Santa Fe Literary Center Book, published by Recursos Press, 826 Camino de Monte Re, Santa Fe, New Mexico 87501.

Manufactured in the United State of America.

ISBN 0-9628999-0-9

SANTA FE LITERARY CENTER BOOKS / RECURSOS PRESS

The poems in this collection first appeared in the following magazines:

Antaeus: Terraces of Rain.
Denver Quarterly: Nights in the Villa.
Field: Francesco and Clare; The Lake.
The Gettysburg Review: Last Night With Rafaella.
The Missouri Review: Vespers: *The Balcony*; Eclogue.
Open Places: The Bells of Santa Maria in Trastevere; The World They Knew; The Photograph of *V* in Venice.
Pequod: The *Kama Sutra* According to Fiat; To Pasolini; Castello (1527).
Poetry: The Doors; From A Daybook.

"Last Night With Rafaella" also appeared in *The Best American Poetry of 1990*.

I would like to thank The American Academy and Institute of Arts and Letters for its award of the Rome Fellowship in Literature. Thanks also to The American Academy in Rome.

—David St. John

First edition.

For Molly

CONTENTS

TERRACES OF RAIN

I.

Ed io riverso
nel potere che grava attorno, cedo
al sortilegio de non riconoscere
di me più nulla fuordi me . . .

—Eugenio Montale

TERRACES OF RAIN

And the mole crept along the garden,
And moonlight stroked the young buds of
The lemon trees, and they walked the five lands . . .
Sheer terraces, rocks rising
Straight up from the sea; the strung vines
Of the grapes, the upraised hands of the olives,
Presided and blessed. Between Vernazza
And Montorosso, along a path
Cut into the sea cliff, a place for lovers
To look down and consider their love,
They climbed up to the double-backed lane
Where a few old women gathered herbs
By the roadside. Voices —
Scattered in the hills above —
Fell like rushes in a wind, their rasp and echo
Traveling down and forever in the clear sea air . . .
Then clouds, then mist, then a universal gray . . .
Where Signore and Signora Bianchini are having lunch,

She stops to talk with them, weather being
The unavoidable topic. Slips of rain, a child's
Scrawl, sudden layers and pages — then, at last,
The fan of sunlight scraping clean
The sky. Here, the world's
Very old, very stubborn, and proud. In the twilight:
Shadow and other, watching the painted foam of
Waves running from the sunset
To the coves, the over-turned skiffs, the white nets
Drying in the reddening air. She stood
Behind him, resting her hand on his shoulder. Night
Spread above them like a circling breeze,
The way a simple memory had once
Returned to Montale, calming his childhood
And a troubled winter sea. The air still cleansing,
She said, the heart that was uncleansable. The unforgiving
One, that heart . . . A boy in an emerald sweater
Passed, out walking a mongrel in good spirits. Across
The scallop of bay, the boats began
Returning to the harbor. Silent. Harsh. Such country
Breaks the selfish heart. There is no original sin:
To be in love is to be granted the only grace
Of all women and all men.

(The Cinque Terre)

FRANCESCO AND CLARE

It was there, in the little town
On top of the mountain, they walked,
Francesco and Chiara,
That's who they were, that's what
They told themselves — a joke, their joke
About two saints, failed lovers held apart
From the world of flesh, Francis and Clare,
Out walking the old city, two saints,
Sainted ones, holy, held close to the life . . .
Poverty, the pure life, the one
Life for Franzikus and Klara,
Stalwarts given
To the joys of God in heaven
And on earth, Mother, praising Brother Sun
And Sister Moon; twin saints, unified
In their beauty as one, Francisco and Clara,
A beauty said of God's will and word, bestowed
And polished by poverty, François
With Claire, the chosen poverty, the true
Poverty that would not be their lives . . .

And they took their favorite names, Clare and Francesco,
Walking the streets of stone the true saints
Walked, watching as the larks swirled
Above the serene towers, the larks
Francesco once described as the color
Of goodness, that is, of the earth, of the dead . . .
Larks who'd not seek for themselves any extravagant
Plumage, humble and simple, God's birds
Twirling and twisting up the pillowing air . . .
And Francesco said to Clare, *Oh little plant I love,*
My eyes are almost blind with Brother Sun . . . tell me,
Who hides inside God's time . . . ?
And Clare, rock of all Poor Clares, stood
In the warm piazza overlooking the valley, weary,
Her shoulder bag sagging from the weight
Of her maps and books, and said across the rain-slick
Asphalt of the parking lot, to the poor bird climbing
The wheel of sky it always had loved best,
Dear lark, dear saint, all my kisses on your nest!

(Assisi)

THE LAKE

At the point of land
That tipped farthest into the lake,
A promontory of ruins and rock, they sat,
Slicing fruit and waving to the Sunday boaters
Zooming over the water in little speedsters.
On the next point: the old villa
Of Catullus, its massive walls and stairways, stables
And baths. It was nice to think of him there,
Walking the narrow beaches below the villa
Where the café was now, where
The woman behind the bar was yelling
Down to her son, chubby in his nylon trunks
And asleep on the sand, a towel only partly
Wrapped around him. Catullus would like her,
Yelling like that, just as he'd like the young man
Leading his pregnant wife and three daughters
Step by step over the rocks, into the water,
To the wide, flat jetty where they stand laughing
As the mild waves run up to wash their feet . . .

And why *should* Catullus go back
To the city, just to watch Lesbia rattle her purse?
Why not stay here by the lake, where her letters
Could be answered leisurely and with the proper venom?
Catullus closed his eyes, imagining the weight
Of her breasts in his hands . . .
Just as the boaters passed, she turned, handing
Over the knife. As he sliced the blood orange, its
Juice ran out around the blade, over his fingers,
Over the rocks and gravel. She leaned
Over to kiss his ear. And the whirr of the motors
Out on the lake was like the roar of bees
To the flowers just opening their damp petals again
After the sudden curtain-fall of a summer's rain.

(Sirmione)

VESPERS: *The Balcony*

They held to the rhythms of the day
In a style less frequent
Than imagined. She was tearing away
The soft, pocked rind of the orange
When the light across the bakery windows
Shivered a little with the clouds,
Though that was just the simple signal
Of the weather being pleased
With itself. The orange was one whose
Blood had mellowed, had mottled
On the rind; a soft leaf of rust
Not to be confused with the real
Passage of time, or other things . . .
She looked down onto the city —
Listen, she said, and the weight
Of the air shifted. A vine less
Strung than they'd first supposed
Dangled at the worn edge of

The railing. Below, as the light
Ribboned the hills, the last monks
Walked deliberately
From their cloisters, and the one
She used to wave at looked up
Just as he turned the final corner
Of the gardens,
                    heading to the chapel
For vespers. *You see,* she said. *You see?*

(Verona)

THE DOORS

The doors were oak, massive . . .
Their panels, bronze. The 12th Century, a good
Century for fear, he thought, standing there
Before them, these doors of the oldest stories,
Parts of which had always been his life,
His many ancient lives —
It was a beautiful garden; he'd been sorry
To leave. When the boys, his sons, quarreled
And the one fell to the other, he searched
The sky, but the sky blew resolute and bronze . . .
Yet what he recalled most of the day
They left, he and she, were the outspread wings
Of the angel, each inscribed with heavy veins
Like the fronds of an enormous feathery
Palm, the plumage of a showgirl,
And the angel's breath, pungent as anise, fine
As the light rising off a mountain lake
In early autumn — *He thought*

Of the squat boat he must sail, the dove
Set loose above the storming waters,
Of the altar on the hillside and his young
Lamb of a son, of the bitter bronze speaking
At last, saying WAIT! . . . how he'd wept,
Waiting as he had always waited, before
These doors, silence . . .
And the doors repeated their stories: good, evil,
All the shavings of testament, or testimony —
Then, in the shifting dark, he saw her
Beginning the dance; though he
Felt his fear cocooned by her beauty as
The veils slowly fell, still, his shoulders ached
With the knowledge of the air ripped
By the falling sword. Her body was smeared
With oils and scents, covered with nothing except
The long silk loincloth
Wrapped haphazardly around her hips. She danced,
Naming for the whole of the King's court

Every temptation worth dying for . . . as
She unwound the silk from her waist, draping
It loosely around his neck, passing
Slowly before every eye, before
Turning to claim her price. Of course, he knew
He should keep his head about this sort of thing,
But as the sweat ran down into his eyes,
He didn't. *O Sainted Zeno, doors of frozen decay*
Polished by pimps and pilgrims with the froth
Of their prayers, O . . . This was
What he had tried to say, but his tongue grew
So swollen and thick. And his head felt so light,
Yet weary, like a baby's, cradled that way
In her delicate white arms.

(Verona; the Church of San Zeno)

LAST NIGHT WITH RAFAELLA

Last night, with Rafaella,

I sat at one of the outside tables
At *Rosati* watching the *ragazzi* on Vespas
Scream through the Piazza del Popolo

And talked again about changing my life,

Doing something meaningful — perhaps
Exploring a continent or discovering a vaccine,
Falling in love or over the white falls
Of a dramatic South American river! —
And Rafaella

Stroked the back of my wrist as I talked,

Smoothing the hairs until they lay as quietly
As wheat before the old authoritarian wind.

Rafaella had just returned from Milano
Where she'd supervised the Spring collection
Of a famous, even notorious, young designer —

A man whose name brought tears to the eyes
Of Contessas, movie stars, and diplomat's wives
Along the Via Condotti or the Rue
Du Faubourg-St-Honoré.

So I felt comfortable there, with Rafaella,
Discussing these many important things, I mean
The spiritual life, and my own
Long disenchantment with the ordinary world.

Comfortable because I knew she was a sophisticated,
Well-travelled woman, so impossible
To shock. A friend who'd
Often rub the opal on her finger so slowly

It made your mouth water,

The whole while telling you what it would be like
To feel her tongue addressing your ear.

And how could I not trust the advice
Of a woman who, with the ball of her exquisite thumb,

Carefully flared rouge along the white cheekbones
Of the most beautiful women in the world?

Last night, as we lay in the dark,
The windows of her bedroom open to the cypress,
To the stars, to the wind knocking at those stiff
Umbrella pines along her garden's edge,
I noticed as she turned slowly in the moonlight

A small tattoo just above her hip bone —

It was a dove in flight or an angel with its
Head tucked beneath its wing,

I couldn't tell in the shadows . . .

And as I kissed this new illumination of her body
Rafaella said, *Do you know how to tell a model?*
In fashion, they wear tattoos like singular beads
Along their hips,
                    but artists' models
Wear them like badges against the daily nakedness,
The way Celestine has above one nipple that
Minute yellow bee and above
The other an elaborate, cupped poppy . . .

I thought about this,

Pouring myself a little wine and listening
To the owls marking the distances, the geometries
Of the dark.
                    Rafaella's skin was
Slightly damp as I ran my fingertip
Along each delicate winged ridge of her
Collarbone, running the harp length of ribs
Before circling the shy angel . . .

And slowly, as the stars
Shifted in their rack of black complexities above,

Along my shoulder, Rafaella's hair fell in coils,

Like the frayed silk of some ancient tapestry,
Like the spun cocoons of the Orient —
Like a fragile ladder

To some whole other level of the breath.

(Rome)

THE *KAMA SUTRA* ACCORDING TO FIAT

Up on the Gianicolo
In cars painfully *piccolo,*

The view is a pretext
When sex is the full text;

Beneath night's starry webbing
All of Rome is out petting.

A Fiat's micro-conditions
Force the oddest positions:

Arms and legs in the air,
As each lover must dare

Those slow, floorless dances
When making advances.

The "baby-shoes" *Cinquecentoes*,
Though only meant to

Go skating down roads
Are now littered with clothes;

And in the grander sedans
There's a groping of hands

That's just as preposterous
Among the quite prosperous.

Still there's nothing obscene
On the sky's black screen,

And nothing appalling
In cars rocking and stalling;

It's all quite delightful,
Out, getting a nightful . . .

And of sexual particulars
In manuals vehicular

By far the best we've got
Is the *Kama Sutra* by Fiat.

CASTELLO (1527)

Where Cellini stood by the angel
Watching the walls of the loggias and palazzi
Slowly licked gold by flame;
                                    where Cellini
Stood by the angel as the cold night
Reddened with wave after wave of smoke, the blush
Of ash settling like a silence over the Tiber;
Where Cellini stood, the angel
Looked out over Rome, that night a city of stone
And fire — the air, seared; the river, blood . . .
Where the angel stood, Cellini
Commanded the cannon, the arc of each cannonball's
White flight like the traced ellipsis of a dead dove
Tossed the length of the table
One night, to amuse Clement, who was amused;
And so Cellini tossed unplucked dove after dove
Into the air, out of the windows, and at some of
The least distinguished guests. And Clement was amused . . .

Yet when the time had come, when that time had finally
Run out, Clement took Cellini by the arm, pointing
To the angel facing the flames of the city,
Then to the Imperials, then to the men by the cannons;
And by the angel staring out over the Tiber
As if it could see the hills of heaven, Cellini turned
To Clement as the clouds of smoke drifted towards
The Castello,
           and Cellini said, Cellini swore:
They will say it was there by his twin
That Cellini, God's living angel, stood like a stone flame
Before the winds and messengers of hell . . .

(Castel Sant 'Angelo; Rome)

NIGHTS IN THE VILLA

Of those nights he spent
    In the villa, he never once
Saw the sun break above the pines,
    Never once, with her. He'd
Have already walked that curved
    Gravel path past the gardener's
Stone house, where, in the late
    Summer, every window open,
He'd hear the gardener's wife
    Snoring like Neptune rising;
Then, he'd come to the gatehouse
    Beside the huge, ornate iron
Gates — ten feet at their peaks —
    And then out into the street
Where the first gray delivery trucks
    Were hauling fruit and flowers,
Fish and meats — their exhaust
    Clouding the blue dawn. He'd
Never really expected much,

It being a difficult time . . .
With her husband away like that,
　　Traveling to Switzerland or
London, calling her so late at night
　　The sleepy maid could barely
Make it up the stairs to knock, to
　　Wake her for the call. She'd
Step from the warm bed, its nest
　　Of covers, pulling on the pale
Green robe, dragging the fork of her
　　Fingers through her black hair —
Awake, nervous, the violet rings still
　　Deepening beneath his eyes, he'd
Look up as she turned to him, opening
　　The door to take her call at
The hall phone outside the bedroom; she'd
　　Try saying something soothing, if
Unintelligible, in her rough English,
　　About his beauty, his silence, or
Perhaps the child-like toss of his
　　Arms . . . Each morning, fastening
His black leather belt in the dark,
　　He'd stand watching the last stars
Just fading to milk in the sky
　　And feel the fatigue of repetition —
The way he'd turn the old claw of a key
　　In her bedroom door, then down

To the garden, the cold bars of the gate . . .
    Hearing still the rasp of pillows,
The sexual pulse of pines, all
    The waves of silk over goose down
As she'd pull herself up on one elbow,
    Snapping back the curls from her eyes,
Almost smiling, as she said not goodbye
    But, always, " Ciao bello. *Ciao* . . . "

(Rome)

THE BELLS OF SANTA MARIA IN TRASTEVERE

All through the night, the owls' calling
Rose into the black limbs of the umbrella pines,
And the bells of Santa Maria rang the hours,

And the half, and the many quarter hours . . .
The pepper of stars dusted the darkened pines
All through the night, and the owls — calling

To one another across the empty gardens
Of the villa — grew silent only as the distant
Bells of Santa Maria rang the hours

Passing quietly in your arms,
In the stilled and broken cradle of your arms,
All through the night. As the owls' calling

Grew near, you rose at last to pull back
The velvet drapes, and through the open windows
The bells of Santa Maria rang each hour

Drawing on towards morning, your leaving,
The pale and simple morning we'd held back
All through the night, against the owls' calling . . .
And then the bells of Santa Maria rang the hour.

(Rome)

ECLOGUE

They left it all, crossing the river, walking high
Into the hills. Clouds pumped over the valley,
The Arno swelled its curves. As they
Reached a sudden crest
Looking down onto the city, the elegant
Villas scattered on the hillsides below, he saw
Through the olive groves — stretched out on a patch
Of grass — a young shepherd, dressed
In white jeans and a red down jacket, watching over
A meandering flock. He heard the boy whistling
To a dog. He thought: Where did I put them, my own
Notched reed pipes? He felt his thighs turn fleecy,
And putting the pipes to his mouth
He played the first notes of "*A New Shepherd's Calendar,*"
And she looked at him, patient and understanding,
Pulling out a book to read as she sat
On the stone bench, turning so the broken
Sunlight fell over her shoulder and onto the page.
In the distance, the sheep moved slowly towards another

Grassy grove. As the wind dropped, he began to play
The notes meant to accompany:
> *After Months of Raine*
>> *Snow and Sleete*
> *Dog, Sheepe, and Man*
>> *Come into Heete*

And when the scent of the wild mint hit
He leaned back against the twisted trunk of an olive,
Seeing everywhere in the fields below
Not the trees and grass, not the shepherd and sheep,
But instead: the airy cells of monks, those cells
Of San Marco painted by Fra Angelico (the frescoes
Somehow fresh as the blood of the stigmata the young
Shepherd had noticed on each palm that morning,
Pulling on gloves before taking out the flock . . .
Though the boy'd decided it was nothing,
Just blisters broken by
The rough handles of the new used Moto Guzzi
Bought from the sister of a dead friend). And yet
As the vision grew and broke, what
Was he seeing? — Not the boy, no, not the shepherd's
Gloved and stained palms, but the wall at the top
Of the stairway . . .
> Angelico's *Annunciation*. . .

An angel whose scalloped, florid wings opened
With a peacock's iridescence. He leaned forward,
On one knee, before her . . . and as she looked
Up from her book, the gray vaults of the sky
Split with light. And, though he proposed
Nothing new, nothing she hadn't already believed,
Still it's true that within her — she knew —
The future that grew was clear,
As clear as the promise of lilies in spring.

(Florence)

FROM A DAYBOOK

The musk of the cemetery

Was like music to the birds
Who smelled it from miles away
Its call
       the spiked

Caskets of the fallen chestnuts
Split and open on
The paths between the stones

The tombs   and all
In all the present was a little
Hymn to be joined in with . . .

And that was the simple goodness
He supposed
That they would be allowed
As sparrows settled around them
Like ash or leaves   like silent snow

All the tombs in the world share
This: you knock

None of the living answer

(Ravenna; in memory of G)

THE WORLD THEY KNEW

That was the world they knew

A little worn at its edges but still
The most faithful of places
For a man and a women who felt they
Had no choice in such matters

Though in the bigger things
The fated things it's true

One had to take what came
Wolf or lamb
              it didn't matter
In the end the shepherd simply walked
Up to you
And put his warm ashen hand
Against your face

Until the world you knew became
One long and unaccountable
Winter's night

Earlier in the day
She'd fallen asleep in the gardens
Of the Villa d'Este
                                giving in finally
To the fatigue of the sleepless night

It was a little past noon
As he folded the sketchbook and looked up
At the lattice of shadow woven over the clouds
A light bristle of afternoon shower

Covered his face

And he was happy calm
So unlike the man in her dream
The one who stood guard at the gate
Of every night she could not bring herself
To enter
            or desire or fall towards

Ever again like those pieces of rain or leaf
Swirling together into the still dilating
Pupil of

The black and uncovered country well

(Tivoli)

THE PHOTOGRAPH OF *V* IN VENICE

In the photograph of *V*
At four, in Venice, she is standing
On a bridge over the Grand Canal,

A bridge that is only
Slightly less blond than she. Below,
Beyond her, the water of the canal

Is a deep violet which, in the glare,
Seems almost black. Beneath a sunhat
Of straw or woven reeds

She is squinting up at the camera,
Her mouth touched by a smile
Of perfect tolerance for the morning,

For the series of staccato snaps
Of the shutter. In the canal,
Two heavy barges are docked to one

Side, waiting to be unloaded of fruits
And grains, cement, and long bolts
Of cloth. Sliding past,

A frail gondola is taking a couple —
Barely visible in the blur of their
Turning to each other

As the photograph was snapped —
To some destination so boring even
The gondelier has forgotten. Just up

From a vaporetto stop, you can see
The low round tables of a café
Arranged in a double line

Overlooking the water, the orange
Tablecloths flapping slightly in the breeze,
The blue-and-white umbrellas above them

Tilted quietly against the wind. Opposite,
At angles over the windows of a hotel,
The mustard-colored awnings lean

Like the painted backs of a child's Tarot
Deck, though not so elaborately latticed
With that scroll work of faint brown —

Cards like the cards she'd placed
Along the baseboard of the hotel room wall,
Face forward: *The Magus, The Fool,*

Ace of Pentacles, The Lovers . . .
The canal takes a bend in the distance,
Disappearing, black water flowing away

The way a child might believe
Time flows, into a past, towards a future
Too uncertain to be held . . .

                      (The white
Wake of a vaporetto spreads across the dawn
Water and, in the mist, fades . . .)

A sight-seeing ferry hunches at its station,
Along its roof the little
White Os of the life preservers, each

With its slash, its single band of red. And
Who, I wonder, rescued this photo
From some stack of old letters, bent dance

Cards, odd, scattered invitations? —
Pieces of past fortune, scripts and figures
Of uncertain, future plays. What does she

Remember of the hotel room? The slim mask
From Carnevale someone bought her? —
Carved from plaster, painted with that heavy

White glaze: one side of its sculpted face,
The lovely smile and open eye of a Princess;
Its other half, the melancholy

Harlequin — down his cheek, from the black
Almond of his eye, two perfect falling tears . . .
The mask sat against the warped mirror

Of the bureau, beside the perfumes and brushes,
The combs and colognes of the Others,
Who bustled about, packing or unpacking, talking

Across the hallways from room to room . . .
And *V* continues
Looking up into the face of the photographer

(I want to ask, *Was it your Mother,*
Or your Father, V?) as if the future was
Something she'd already forgiven,

Just a moment ago, when a dove fell from
A tower of the palazzo just beyond the bridge,
Landing very deliberately and with its wings

Outspread, to peck at the blond stones
Laid out in their dark mortar
Like planets in the night. And sometimes, in early

Morning, turning to you still asleep
Beside me, sunlight filling the unshaded window,
I want to hold back the black of

That canal, to stop the violet water leading
Past the bend and into every unforgiven year;
I want to touch and freeze

The glare burning at the edge of the lens,
Burning still this *someone*, this child in a photograph,
Burning still this woman I know, this young woman

The child has always known.

II.

      . . . Ma io, con il cuore consciente

di chi soltanto nella storia ha vita,
potrò mai più con pura passione operare,
se so che la nostra storia è finita?

                —Pier Paolo Pasolini
                    (1922-1975)

TO PASOLINI

I. *At Italo's*

Out in the visible city, the heart
Of the night spreads its soft
Black petals. Slowly, the *ragazzi* start

Moving along the streets. A few drift off
Into the piazza below, trading
Cigarettes, phone numbers, jokes. The exhaust

Of Roman traffic thins . . . and finally fades.
The girls, shaking their heads of loose curls;
The boys, exhaling like they've got it made.

Up in Italo's apartment, planets of ice swirl
In my glass, opaque and tinted gold
By the scotch. The room is the color of pearl.

Pier Paolo, Italo tells about the butcher's kid
You picked up the night you died, the bruise
Left along the sallow, broad

Curve of your cheek. Italo says you cruised
Every night of your life — that test
A man makes in the dark. Does any man get used

To the test? If so, not to the scent of death
Hardening in the air like Roman dust,
Stealing its rhythm from every broken breath,

Leaving a shirt flaked with rust,
No, blood and bits of. . . . we know the rest;
We know almost as much as we must —

We know most things hurt; we know this best.
Italo turns to me and says, "Every night of
His life . . . he spent out in the wilderness."

II. *Ostia*

The orphans of the heart must turn to thee
Byron said of Rome, though he could have meant
The way they turned to you, as easily.

The boys standing outside the station have spent
Their last *lire*. Looking for more, looking tough,
One joins you to Ostia, where you often went.

The seaplane basin fills quietly with shadow.
Your immaculate gray Alfa sits a few
Moments, hood still warm, motor switched off . . .

Starlight litters the slowly falling dew;
A man falls to his hands and shattered knees.
The sky streaks with violet veins, then blue.

Mama. Mama. They are killing me . . .

III. *1984*

Last night at dinner at *Vecchia Roma*,
Downing *fettucine ai carciofi*
With my favorite bottle of Boggio,

A young woman I didn't know turned to me —
She was a friend of the friend whose birthday
We'd been celebrating, her hand on my knee

Like an old lover's — and what could I say
When she asked about you, whom I'd never known?
Yet something took me over, the way

In a dream one suddenly feels at home
In even the oddest circumstances. I talked
Endlessly, just the two of us alone,

About those last few days before your death,
Your murder . . . This morning, at my study —
Hungover, depressed — I tried to clear my head

With cup after cup of black, muddied
Espresso. I went out and stood with my back
To the old Aurelian wall, the funny

Garden stretched out below me. The arced black
Limbs of the umbrella pines, all lined
With sparrows; lizards, dancing along the stacks

Of the white bricks. I watched that first fine
Resurrection of the mist just rising
In the early haze of the morning sunlight . . .

Then it hit me, like a simple fist clenched
Against the fact, against the earth —
Last night had been November the second,

The ninth anniversary of your death.

IV. *Una Vita Violenta (1955)*

Many children in only one bed,
An outdoor toilet, a typical Roman slum
Where half of the sons end up in jail or dead

By the time they're fifteen. To get ahead
In this life you can't be as dumb
As the other boys beside you in the bed,

The brothers who cry simply to be fed,
Who cry until adolescence comes,
Then end up in jail or dead.

Some get lucky. In the park, given head
By some prosperous client, they roll him,
Or become one of the few in his bed,

Living longer this way, staying fed
And clothed, even having a little fun
Before going to jail or ending up dead.

They're all my boys, Pier Paolo said,
From the streets and the gutters and the slums;
So many to save from the Tiber's cold bed —

Then God divides: These to jail, these dead.

V. *The Art of Argument, The Argument of Art*

Before our lunch, lovely G tries to explain
How it works with Roman artists of *any*
Kind — writers, sculptors, directors — "Pains

In the ass, all of them; but I swear not many
Were as stubborn as Pier Paolo. Once,
He and T" (her husband) "argued three days running;

First one, then the other, taking his stance
About *'Theater'* — for T, it was art;
For Pier Paolo, art didn't stand a chance.

He said theater should play its part
As a political tool, 'a necessary vehicle
To educate and liberate.' So they'd both start

Shouting at each other, ridiculing
The other's position; only, when it got very late,
Pier Paolo'd go home to sleep — he was no fool —

But! He'd be back early! He couldn't *wait*
To begin the argument again. Still, after
Three days, they both quit. Pasolini walked straight

Out the door and never, I mean not once *ever*
Did he and T speak. It was just nuts;
Two close friends so furious with each other

They go the rest of their lives without
Talking — *or* arguing — for all those years. Dull?
No; but Roman grudges! What a way to live out

One's life, eh? Paranoid, bitter, just enough
Fame to be smug, which is already too much.
It's true not all of us have it so rough;

Besides, an artist's life is always such
Pleasant torture here in Rome, who'd want
To be elsewhere? Now, how about some lunch?"

First, I pour us more wine to drink.
She sighs, then shrugs: "You see,
We argue about really everything we think —

I think it's how we learn what we believe."

VI. *Winter Sun*

It's mid-December in Rome, yet the sun's
Been blazing all week. The air's brisk,
Chilly, then very cold at night when,

If the sky is clear, the clouds all whisked
Away, the searing constellations beat down.
Some mornings, leaves flare and burn like old lists

Out by the gardener's shed. Along the lawn,
The paths marked by low shrubs rustle and whine
With lizards as I pass. Azaleas, newly blown,

Rock in the flower beds. The quiet pines,
Stately and aloof, fill yet again with sparrows.
Each afternoon, I pour a glass of wine

And watch those sparrows fall and swoop above
Some morsel of worm or bug. From the cracks
In the Aurelian wall, the lizards come

Crawling onto the bleached bricks, to bask
In the steady sun. They have nothing to fear;
At least, nothing but the quick shadow cast

As I lean back in my chair. It's quiet here,
Away from the farting Vespas and the acrid
City air. I look over the garden, where

The smoke of the burning leaves still drifts
Above the heads of the wildflowers. *To
Live is to struggle, to struggle is to live —*

That's what you said. Pier Paolo, whose
                 Love are we so terrified to lose?

VII. *Hotel of Ash*

The hotel room is tawdry, non-descript;
There is a narrow cot, a straight-backed chair,
A dresser with a huge mirror that barely fits

Between the single window and the closet door.
The boy pulls the chair right up to the dresser,
Reaching out to tilt the beveled mirror

Until he sits before his image, there —
Reflected. He waits. The room reeks and sways.
He flips his cigarette butt into the air,

Toward the old tin of ashes, and says
To no one, "*Bless me, Father* . . . " He picks up
The worn muslin curtain, where it lies

Crumpled on the floor; he spreads it out.
He scatters the ashes from the cigarette tin
And rubs them slowly over the whole cloth

Until the muslin has been blackened
Like a mourning veil. Over the low, angled
Image of himself he drapes the ashen curtain,

And sits back again in the mangled,
Rickety chair. Its wood, completely scarred
By knifed initials, burns. His face, an angel's

Reflected in the quiet of the mirror,
Though now only faintly visible
Behind the dark muslin, the hung, tarred

Veil of his home-made confessional.
Behind its curtain, in the silver glass,
The Angel of Forgiveness is reasonable,

And waiting. Waiting for this silence
To be broken, for the boy at the dresser
To begin his story of concluding violence.

He shrugs and, as if still without a care,
Lights another cigarette. The breeze
From the window mutters in the ashen air;

Angel-breath, mirror-fog: the man's pleas
As the board smashes against his head —
The Alfa no longer purring like the sea . . .

The boy continues until Pasolini's nearly dead,
Then gets into the lean gray car
And backs over him, then forward, across his head.

Now the boy lifts his eyes to this horror
Of himself: the mask of the dead angel
Hanging before him in the blowing mirror . . .

The face of Pasolini pulsing on the skull
Where the boy's own face should be —
Confessor, and victim. The rippling veil

Torn between the two worlds. The sea
Slapping the coast of Ostia, the seaplane
Basin quiet now. The murmuring gray

Alfa, the boy at the wheel, turns toward dawn,
Toward Rome . . . the corpse jerks once or twice.
And Pasolini's ghost smirks: *"Cut. Cut. FIN!"*

Here, the scene suffers its awkward splice —
The boy's head falls forward onto his chest.
Days roll slowly in the sky, black dice . . .

Pasolini said he'd never die like the rest;
I'm not sure *this* is what he meant.
Though, possibly . . . the ash, its blunt kiss

Still printed on his cheek . . . the wood, bent.
What better place to die than near the sea?
Which coins still left to spill? Which spent?

VIII. *Love for the Dragon*

History is blood; or so history says.
There are some lessons we'd rather not learn.
For Pasolini, the question was, each day:

How does one live? What can one *do*, I mean.
He believed beliefs should be fiercely held,
This most public of private men —

One must: 1) Love poetry after poetry's death;
2) Remain *of* the spirit without a God;
3)Trust always in the beauty of the raw;

4) Meld the contemplative with the active world;
5) Piss stylishly in the face of repression;
6) Simply refuse to be bored;

7) Wildly annihilate one's own reputation;
8) Go out every night
Religiously, taking the body's dictation;

9) Regard history as the soul's spotlight,
And fix one's place in its theater;
10) Never forget what it meant to be truly poor.

Who could think of anything better?
Except perhaps to remain,
As Pasolini wished to, the child of this letter:

Dear _____: Sitting by the small stone fountain
At the Villa Sciarra, with a little time to spend;
The white wisteria's slowly blooming again

On the laced arbor above — winter's end,
At last. A boy in green khaki shorts just passed,
Followed by his mother and her "friend,"

A man too suave, too slick, too crass
To be the boy's father. Besides, the boy
Paid no attention to him at all, this last

Of his mother's men. The boy dragged an old toy
Dragon behind him on a short gold cord,
Its mouth spitting little friction sparks of joy —

He circled the fountain like a tiny Chinese lord,
Secure in his wild love for the dragon,
Its steady metallic pulse all that any of us heard.

His mother called out to him, as did her "friend;"
Yet they, like the world, were triumphantly ignored.
Ah, I thought, to be *that* powerful! To have again,

As a boy, a dragon on a leash! And to be heard
In one's own pure defiant silence —
To have again a dragon's voice; I mean, that is . . .
                                        the last word.

NOTES

The quote from Eugenio Montale comes from his poem "Due nel crepuscolo," from his book LA BUFERA E ALTRO (Arnoldo Mondadori Editore; 1957). In William Arrowsmith's translation (THE STORM AND OTHER THINGS, Norton; 1985), the passage reads:

> And I, overwhelmed
> by the power weighing around us, yield
> to the sorcery of no longer knowing anything
> outside myself . . .

The passage by Pasolini concludes his famous elegy "Le ceneri di Gramsci" from the book of the same title (Aldo Garzanti Editore; 1957). In Norman MacAfee's translation (PIER PAOLO PASOLINI: POEMS, Random House; 1982), the passage reads:

> But I with the conscious heart
>
> of one who can live only in history,
> will I ever again be able to act with pure passion
> when I know our history is over?

DAVID ST. JOHN is the author of three collections of poetry, *HUSH* (1976), *THE SHORE* (1980), and *NO HEAVEN* (1985), as well as two limited edition books, *THE OLIVE GROVE* (1980) and *THE ORANGE PIANO* (1987). He has received grants and fellowships from The John Simon Guggenheim Memorial Foundation, The National Endowment for the Arts, The Ingram Merrill Foundation, and The Maryland Arts Council. *HUSH* was awarded the Great Lakes College Association Prize as the best first book of 1976; *THE SHORE* was awarded The James D. Phelan Prize from The San Francisco Foundation. In 1984, Mr. St. John received the Prix de Rome Fellowship in Literature, awarded by The American Academy and Institute of Arts and Letters. He is Poetry Editor of *The Antioch Review* and Professor of English at The University of Southern California.

ANTOINE PREDOCK is a noted architect whose main studio is in Albuquerque, New Mexico. Predock studied at Columbia and the University of New Mexico. After graduating from Columbia, he was granted a traveling fellowship to Spain. His career has included Visiting Professorships at a number of universities, including Harvard, Clemson, the University of Maryland, and currently at the University of California, Los Angeles. In 1985 he was a Fellow at the American Academy in Rome. The drawings included in this volume were completed in Italy at that time.

THE DRAWINGS OF ANTOINE PREDOCK: